Solutions for Modern Learning

Freedom to Learn

Will Richardson

Solution Tree | Press

a division of
Solution Tree

Copyright © 2016 by Solution Tree Press

All rights reserved, including the right of reproduction of this book in whole or in part in any form.

555 North Morton Street
Bloomington, IN 47404
800.733.6786 (toll free) / 812.336.7700
FAX: 812.336.7790
email: info@solution-tree.com
solution-tree.com

Printed in the United States of America

19 18 17 16 15   2 3 4 5

Library of Congress Control Number: 2015944699

Solution Tree
Jeffrey C. Jones, CEO
Edmund M. Ackerman, President

Solution Tree Press
President: Douglas M. Rife
Associate Acquisitions Editor: Kari Gillesse
Editorial Director: Lesley Bolton
Managing Production Editor: Caroline Weiss
Production Editor: Tara Perkins
Proofreader: Jessi Finn
Text Designer: Rian Anderson
Cover Designers: Rian Anderson and Abigail Bowen

Table of Contents

About the Author

 A parent of two teenagers, **Will Richardson** has spent the last dozen years developing an international reputation as a leading thinker and writer about the intersection of social online learning networks and education. He was one of a handful of original education bloggers (http://willrichardson .com), and his work has appeared in numerous journals, newspapers, and magazines, such as *Educational Leadership*, *District Administration*, *Education Week*, the *New York Times*, and *English Journal*. He is an outspoken advocate for change in schools and classrooms in the context of the diverse, new learning opportunities that the web and other technologies now offer.

Will has authored five books, most recently *From Master Teacher to Master Learner* (2015, Solution Tree Press). In total, his books have sold more than two hundred thousand copies worldwide.

A former public school educator of twenty-two years, Will is a cofounder of Modern Learner Media and copublisher of Educating Modern Learners (http://modernlearners.com), which is a site dedicated to helping educational leaders and policy makers develop new contexts for conversations around education. Over the past eight years, he has spoken to tens of thousands of educators in more than a dozen countries about the merits of online learning networks for personal and professional growth. Will lives in rural New Jersey with his wife, Wendy, and his children, Tess and Tucker.

To book Will Richardson for professional development, contact pd@solution-tree.com.

Preface

In the 1960s and 1970s, Penguin published a series of what it called *education specials*, short books from a variety of authors such as Neil Postman, Ivan Illich, Herb Kohl, Paulo Freire, Jonathan Kozol, and others. All told, there were more than a dozen works, and they were primarily edgy, provocative essays meant to articulate an acute dissatisfaction with the function of schools at the time. The titles reflected that and included books such as *The Underachieving School, Compulsory Mis-Education and the Community of Scholars, Teaching as a Subversive Activity, Deschooling Society,* and *School Is Dead,* to name a few. Obviously, the messages of these books were not subtle.

Progressive by nature, the authors generally saw their schools as unequal, undemocratic, and controlling places of conformity and indoctrination. They argued, mostly to nonlistening ears, that traditional school narratives were leaving their learners disengaged and lacking in creativity and curiosity, and the systems and structures of schools were deepening instead of ameliorating the inequities in society. A number of the authors argued that universal schooling was a pipe dream from both economic and political perspectives, and schools, if they were to remain, needed to be rethought from the ground up.

Reading many of these works now, it's hard not to be struck by how precisely they describe many of the realities of today's world. It's inarguable that an education in the United States (and elsewhere) remains vastly unequal among socioeconomic groups and various races and ethnicities. The systems that drove schools years ago prevail and, in many cases, are less and less economically viable by the day. By and large, education is something still organized, controlled, and delivered by the institution; very little agency or autonomy is afforded to the learner over his or her own learning. Decades of reform efforts guided principally by politicians and businesspeople have failed to enact the types of widespread changes that those Penguin authors and many others felt were needed for schools to serve every learner equally and adequately in preparing him or her for the world that lies ahead.

It's the "world that lies ahead" that is the focus of this book, part of the *Solutions for Modern Learning* series. Let us say up front that we in no way assume that these books will match the intellectual heft of those writers in the Penguin series (though we hope to come close). However, we aspire to reignite or perhaps even start some important conversations about change in schools, given the continuing longstanding challenges from decades past as well as the modern contexts of a highly networked, technology-packed, fast-changing world whose future looks less predictable by the minute.

Changes in technology since the early 1990s, and specifically, the Internet, have had an enormous impact on how we communicate, create, and most importantly, learn. Nowhere have those effects been felt more acutely than with our learners, most of whom have never known a world without the Internet. In almost all areas of life, in almost every institution and society, the effects of ubiquitously connected technologies we now carry with us in our backpacks and back pockets have been profound, creating amazing opportunities and complex challenges, both of which have been hard to foresee. In no uncertain terms, the world has changed and continues to change quickly and drastically.

Yet, education has remained fairly steadfast, pushing potentially transformative learning devices and programs to the edges, never allowing them to penetrate to the core of learning in schools.

Learning in schools looks, sounds, and feels pretty much like it did in the 1970s, if not in the early 1900s.

Here's the problem: increasingly, for those who have the benefit of technology devices and access to the Internet, learning outside of school is more profound, relevant, and long lasting than learning inside the classroom. Connected learners of all ages have agency and autonomy that are stripped from them as they enter school. In a learning context, this is no longer the world that schools were built for, and in that light, it's a pretty good bet that a fundamental redefinition of school is imminent.

While some would like to see schools done away with completely, we believe schools can play a crucially important role in the lives of our youth, the fabric of our communities, and the functioning of our nations. But moving forward, we believe schools can only play these roles if we fully understand and embrace the new contexts that the modern world offers for learning and education. This is not just about equal access to technology and the Internet, although that's a good start. This is about seeing our purpose and our practice through a different lens that understands the new literacies, skills, and dispositions that students need to flourish in a networked world. Our hope is that the books in the *Solutions for Modern Learning* series make that lens clearer and more widespread.

Introduction: Blueprints for Learning

What does education often do? It makes a straight-cut ditch of a free, meandering brook.

—Henry David Thoreau

Sophomore Jeremy Dortch has a huge roll of blueprints under his arm, and as he navigates across his classroom at Castle View High School in Colorado, it's all he can do to bend his way around fellow students and computer desks and the occasional teacher without knocking into them. With his free hand, he signals across the room to a maintenance man who is standing next to a solitary, off-white square pole with a capped-off junction box at the bottom. It's smack in the center of the room, and it's about to be transformed.

"I'm Jeremy," he says as he extends his hand to the somewhat befuddled-looking middle-aged man looking at the pole.

"Ron," the man says without looking at him. "Now, what's the problem here?"

"Oh, no problem," Jeremy replies. "It's just that we wanted to make sure the power was shut off when the construction guys get here Monday to start building the walls."

Ron looks up. "Walls? What walls?"

"These walls," Jeremy says as he drops to his knees and rolls out some architectural drawings of the classroom. He points to some blue lines. "Right here."

Ron glances down and squints. "But Monday is the first day of break . . . no one's even going to be here."

Jeremy smiles. "Well, we will. We'll be here all next week helping and redecorating. So if you could shut the electricity to this pole off for us before you leave today, I'd really appreciate it."

Ron looks even more confused. "So wait, you're going to be here? In the classroom? During break?"

"Yep," Jeremy says. "A bunch of us are helping with the construction. It's all here in the blueprints if you want to see them."

Ron looks down to the stack of drawings on the floor. "Will there be a teacher here?"

"Mr. Schneider and about six other students will be here," Jeremy says. He jerks his thumb over his shoulder and asks, "You want to talk to him?"

Ron glances up and eyes the teacher, then looks back at the pole. "Who capped off the electricity here?" He points to the silver plate where an outlet used to be.

"Well, I did," Jeremy says. "I got permission."

"You an electrician?" Ron asks, looking the boy in the eye.

"No, but I learned how to do it."

"Well, now," Ron says slowly, "who taught you how to do that?"

Starting Points

How do we learn most powerfully and deeply in our lives? Over the past decade or so, I've been shocked at how little we pay attention to this fundamental question in the context of schools. It is rare that I visit a school where conversations about what powerful learning is and how it actually takes place are held on an ongoing basis. Only occasionally have I seen that question be the starting point for decisions regarding curriculum, classroom design, technology purchases, pedagogy, assessments, staffing, and more. It's difficult, in fact, to find a school where all the teachers, administrators, and students can articulate a consistent vision of how learning happens most effectively in classrooms even though the most stated goal in education seems to be to "improve student learning," at least the type that's easy to measure by standardized assessments.

The irony is that almost every one of you reading this book, whether you are an educator, a parent, a policymaker, or just an interested observer, knows the answer to that question. Each of us need only reflect on what we ourselves have learned most powerfully and deeply in our own lives to craft a response. And I would bet that the consistency in the answers we give would astonish us. We've learned most deeply those things that we truly cared about, those things that had relevance in our lives. We've learned those things with other people with whom we shared that interest. We've learned them haphazardly; rarely is there a fixed or linear path. And we've learned best what we've applied in some way in our lives. In other words, understanding how powerful learning happens isn't rocket science. We're all learners, and we know what it means to learn.

Though we in education are loathe to admit it, however, our dilemma in schools has always been the disconnect between the way we learn naturally in our day-to-day lives and the way we approach learning in schools. To put it bluntly, we know how learning happens in real life, yet we seem to ignore that when we step into the classroom. Few put it as succinctly as author and educator Seymour Papert (1993), who has become one of my biggest influences and teachers about learning:

> When it comes to thinking about learning, nearly all of us have a school side of the brain, which thinks that school is the only natural way to learn, and the personal side

which knows perfectly well it's not. . . . Every one of us
has built up a stock of intuitive, empathic, commonsense knowledge about learning. (p. 28)

For the last 150 years, the narrative that schools are the places that
we go to learn the things we need to be successful in life has grown
deep, deep roots. The majority of people in the developed world
have looked to schools for an education, and we've adopted what
author Frank Smith (1998) calls the "official theory of learning" that
our systems promote. Smith (1998) writes that this "official theory"
is an extremely powerful one:

It is a theory that learning is work, and that anything
can be learned provided sufficient effort is expended
and sufficient control enforced. The theory has gained
supreme power in educational systems from kindergarten to university. It has become so pervasive that
many people can't imagine an alternative to it. (p. 4)

Smith (1998) calls this "official" view "totally artificial, a theory con-
trived solely for the purposes of control" (p. 4). And since the form
and function of current schools evolved from the techniques used
by the 19th century Prussian army to train soldiers, techniques that
were then applied to preparing a 20th century industrial workforce
at scale, it shouldn't surprise us that much of the school experience
is about control. A school's view of an "education" is one that is
clearly defined, efficient to enact, easy to measure, and applicable to
all. While in our heart of hearts we know that school-based learning
flies in the face of our "commonsense knowledge about learning,"
it's a powerful mix of tradition, policy, and nostalgia that keeps it
firmly in place.

But there is, as we know, another way to think about learning.
Smith (1998) calls it the "classic theory," one that is closer to what
we know it looks like in our own lives:

It is classic because it is archetypal, universal, deeply rooted, and uncontaminated. It says, very simply,
that we learn from the people around us with whom

> we identify. We can't help learning from them, and
> we learn without knowing that we are learning . . .
> Learning is continual, effortless, unpremeditated,
> independent of rewards and punishment, a social ac-
> tivity, all about growth, and never forgotten. (pp. 3, 6)

If that gives you pause, think of any four-year-old you've ever seen on a playground or in a home surrounded by toys. Or think of the members of any athletic team or musical group. Think of a team of scientists engaged in solving a challenging problem. Or, again, think of your own learning.

I'm not suggesting that there's anything earth-shatteringly new here. Jean Piaget and John Dewey and Maria Montessori and Lev Vygotsky and a whole host of others have been talking and writing about this for more than a century. That we learn by doing, that learning happens through play, that learning can't be forced, that learning is real life—these ideas and more have formed the foundation for a progressive view of education that has struggled to gain credence in a world where the idea of highly organized and standardized schooling has become pervasive. In fact, one could argue that the systems and structures of schools have effectively repelled those progressive ideas in a form of self-preservation.

By and large, the classic theory that describes our own best learning is not the way we conceptualize what student learning should look like in schools. But here's our challenge: if schools are to remain at all relevant in our kids' lives, it's becoming increasingly clear that we're going to have to start embracing the classic theory inside the classroom walls, and the sooner the better.

What's New

Why do we need to reconceptualize learning in school? Because something incredibly important has happened in the last fifteen years in human history when it comes to learning: the web and an array of accompanying technologies have created a totally new world of possibilities for us to learn and create and connect. This still relatively new thing we call the Internet contains an unfathomable amount of information and knowledge, billions of people who serve as potential teachers in our lives, and an untold number of tools for connecting and creating that were unimaginable just a few years ago. And my thesis in writing this book is simply this: If we have access to the Internet, and if we have the skills, literacies, and dispositions to use it well, we now have a vastly expanded *freedom to learn* that (1) fundamentally challenges the traditional narratives and structures of schooling, (2) requires us to completely rethink the student outcomes that our schools aspire to, and (3) demands a more progressive or classic approach to learning in our schools if they are to remain germane.

The reality today—in the developed world, at least—is that a fast-growing number of our students are using their access to pursue powerful and meaningful learning opportunities on demand with people they don't know, around the things they want or need to learn, in ways that have little resemblance to how they are expected to learn in school (where they have little if any freedom to do that). Those opportunities are exploding, and, importantly, these new technologies amplify our ability to, as Smith says, "learn from the people around us with whom we identify."

When some of the smartest contemporary minds in education like Seymour Papert, Christopher Dede, Sugata Mitra, Bette Manchester, and about twenty others got together in Maine in 2010 at what was called the Big Ideas Global Summit, this is how they articulated this shift:

> What is becoming better understood is what personal computing in the hands of learners allows. The emphasis is more about who controls the learning than about content. It's about learners learning through the lens of topics and issues that are of interest, relevant and purposeful to them; it's about them constructing knowledge; it's about connecting to an unlimited re-

> source of people, ideas, and conversations that gives all learners unique insights, insights that underpin deeper understandings about the world in which they live, and how they might act collectively to influence their world and their lives. It's about having the freedom to learn in a way that is appropriate in a modern world. It's about acknowledging a learner's innate drive to learn about, and understand, his or her place in the world. (Dixon & Einhorn, 2011, p. 11)

In other words, access to the Internet and powerful computing devices fundamentally changes things when it comes to what our kids can learn and create.

But that freedom to learn that our kids (and we ourselves) enjoy outside the school walls is almost universally taken away inside the school walls. Again, this is not a necessarily modern development. Back in the early 1970s, Ivan Illich (1971) wrote *Deschooling Society* (one of the books that inspired this series, in fact) and said, "For most men the right to learn is curtailed by the obligation to attend school" (p. 2). And even in a modern context, I'm not talking so much about the restrictions placed on phones and computers and connections that our kids carry with them (or that we give them) as much as I'm talking about the stripping of agency and autonomy over the learning process. Schools "work" in the traditional sense because they are the organizing structures for delivering an education. Students are organized by age into discipline-specific classrooms. Lessons are planned and checked. Assessments are taken and recorded. Grades are used to determine the success or failure of any individual student's attempts at navigating what the system puts in front of them and the opportunities that student has for either college or work. As I alluded to earlier, schools, by nature and by law, control every piece of the learning experience. And we don't just take away a freedom to learn; we restrict expression with dress codes, put limits on publication and speech, and even define the amount of affection students can show for one another. Almost every aspect of a student's participation in school is subject to some control in the service of efficiency and order.

To some extent, I understand why we did this. The idea of "educating" every child required a great deal of oversight and efficiency. Our school structures were designed primarily to help the institution do its work, not to help students have the best possible environment for learning. Few would argue that separating students by age is best for them, but it's no doubt easier for us to manage the experience if we do. When we operate under the worldview that a child has to attend a school in order to access information, knowledge, teachers, and everything else education related, it's no wonder we made the system highly organized and standardized.

In a learning context, however, what the web has created is a challenging conundrum for those who hold that traditional vision of what role schools play in educating students and how that education should be meted out. Assuming access, which is admittedly a big assumption, learning on the web is limited only by our level of desire and our lack of literacy. Learners of all ages now have almost complete agency over the what, how, when, and who of learning in ways that didn't exist a generation ago. Access to and the sharing of information are now virtually uncontrollable. Margaret Weigel, Carrie James, and Howard Gardner (2009) of the Harvard Graduate School of Education describe it this way:

> A motivated learner can investigate a wide variety of personal interests on his or her own. Or potentially, he or she can learn sophisticated analytic and social skills by playing complex games or participating in a social network or online forum, entirely independent of formal educational experiences or designated instructors.

Read that last part again: "entirely independent of formal educational experiences or designated instructors." That, in a nutshell, is the daunting new reality for those holding to a traditional mindset around schools and education.

That doesn't mean, however, that we get rid of schools or teachers just because the vast majority of the curriculum that we currently teach and thousands (if not millions) of potentially powerful mentors are now available through a few clicks on our mobile devices. As Weigel et al. (2009) go on to say:

> The Internet's potential for learning may be curtailed if youth lack key skills for navigating it, if they consistently engage with Internet resources in a shallow fashion, and/or if they limit their explorations to a narrow band of things they believe are worth knowing. Left to their own devices and without sufficient scaffolding, student investigations may turn out to be thoughtful and meaningful—or frustrating and fruitless. A successful informal learning practice depends upon an independent, constructivistically oriented learner who can identify, locate, process, and synthesize the information he or she is lacking.

That, in fact, is where the incredibly valuable roles of schools and teachers now reside, *in developing each student's potential to learn on his or her own, without us.* In that, I think it's arguable that the need for schools and teachers is even more important today because developing as an "independent, constructivistically oriented learner" is much more complex and nuanced than becoming someone who knows a lot of stuff and can recall it for a test.

In this moment, the defining question for educators is this: Now that students have abundant access to knowledge, information, teachers, and technologies online, what's more important: making sure students master a school-designed curriculum that covers only a fraction of everything that's now knowable? Or making sure that students have the ability to learn deeply and powerfully in the real world *on their own, freely,* without the mediating function of the institution?

How each of us answers it defines our work moving forward. In fact, I think it's arguable that it may define the future of the world. (No pressure.)

In the pages that follow, I want to tease out why bringing that freedom to learn inside the classroom walls is an imperative to the future of our community schools (as well as schools in general) and to the success and well-being of our kids. I have two of them, both teenagers, so my desire to help all kids find success in their lives is personal as well as professional. But it's not as simple as honoring a freedom to learn. It's also about a freedom to teach, a culture and a society that promote a freedom to learn, and the accompanying literacies and structures that make all of that possible. On its face, a discussion about what promotes deep and powerful learning should be simple, but there's no question that in the context of schools, it's a highly complex conversation.

This is not an easy conversation for me. I'm a product of traditional public schools. I taught and was an administrator in a traditional public school for twenty-two years. Many of my friends are traditional public school teachers. I believe in the ideal of public schools, and I believe that despite the huge changes we are experiencing in learning via technology, schools still have a viable, important role to play in preparing our kids for the worlds they will inhabit. I refuse to believe, as others do, that we should just bulldoze the idea of schooling as it stands and start fresh. As my friend author and educator Gary Stager (n.d.) says, "schools are where the kids are," and we can't give up in our efforts to rewrite the traditional scripts instead of simply tossing them aside. Such thinking and rhetoric ignore the realities of millions of kids who can't wait for those new concepts of schooling to materialize. And in most cases, the current definition of *fresh* is little more than a different way of putting a more colorful technological wrapping and bow around traditional outcomes in ways that make more money for the curriculum and assessment corporations framing those visions in the first place.

Make no mistake, rewriting this script will be enormously difficult, and I'm going to detail some of the barriers in a later chapter. I wouldn't doubt that already, many of you reading this are connecting intellectually to these old and new realities about learning but feel at a total loss about what to do about them practically. In the end, it may be impossible to change learning in schools at scale, especially to the level that I'm going to advocate for here. But my hope is that after reading this book, you'll agree that the realities of the modern world absolutely require a rethinking of the roles of schools and teachers in our kids' lives and that we absolutely must begin to craft new stories and narratives around what it means to learn in school, what it means to be "educated," and what we need every child to know and be able to do in order to flourish in his or her own life. My hope is that you'll see the deep connection between the amazing new affordances to learn with the web and the common sense—personal knowledge that we all have about learning but choose to ignore in schools—and engage in new, ongoing conversations around practice in your own schools and districts.

Chapter 1
The Current System

Let's take a look at the effectiveness of the current system as a starting point for talking about change. No question, some schools are more "successful" than others when it comes to the traditional ways we assess such things (test scores, graduation rates, and so on). There is little argument any longer that we are effectively failing our children who live in poverty and are under duress from a host of societal inequalities. But in general, it's also becoming harder to argue that the current practice of schooling is serving even our most fortunate and well-off children as well as it needs to be. In the United States, we may be graduating a higher percentage of students than we have in the past, but it's what happens to those students that is relevant for this discussion. In short, we have a number of problems, including low student engagement, low retention of learning, and a misguided idea of what constitutes success.

Low Engagement

First and foremost, it's hard to deny that the current system of schooling curtails our students' interest in learning. Nowhere is that more evident than in the results of a 2012 Gallup survey of student engagement in K–12 schools (Busteed, 2013). This was no small study—500,000 kids from 1,700 public schools in 37 states. What

Gallup found was that by high school, only four in ten of our children reported being engaged in school. Four in ten. Are we OK with that number? The author of the Gallup article states, "Our educational system sends students and our country's future over the school cliff every year" (Busteed, 2013). If you want even more cause for concern, a subsequent Gallup poll showed that 70 percent of teachers in America were classified as "disengaged" (Kamenetz, 2014). Or look at another survey done by former superintendent Lee Jenkins (2012), who found that 95 percent of kindergarten kids love school but only 37 percent of high school sophomores do. I can't imagine any of us would consider that a success.

In addition, take College of William and Mary professor and researcher Kyung Hee Kim's 2013 report documenting a continuous decline in creativity among American schoolchildren over the last two or three decades. According to Kim's research:

> Children have become less emotionally expressive, less energetic, less talkative and verbally expressive, less humorous, less imaginative, less unconventional, less lively and passionate, less perceptive, less apt to connect seemingly irrelevant things, less synthesizing, and less likely to see things from a different angle. (as cited in Chao & Lopez-Gottardi, 2015)

According to psychologist Peter Gray (2012), the causes for that are obvious:

> Creativity is nurtured by freedom and stifled by the continuous monitoring, evaluation, adult-direction, and pressure to conform that restrict children's lives today. In the real world few questions have one right answer, few problems have one right solution; that's why creativity is crucial to success in the real world. But more and more we are subjecting children to an educational system that assumes one right answer to every question and one correct solution to every problem, a system that punishes children (and their teachers too) for daring to try different routes.

In other words, with the advent of more standardization, more curriculum, and more testing, our kids have become less and less free. The consequences are devastating.

Now, I know some of you reading will say, "Well, that's not my school . . . our kids are creative and engaged." Fair enough. Perhaps you or your students weren't studied. But what do we say, then, to Dave Cormier (2014), a professor at the University of Prince Edward Island, when he writes:

> The vast majority of students coming to most universities are not prepared to be engaged in learning. It's that simple. It crosses socio-economic barriers. It crosses cultural differences. We are not bringing up a generation of children who are ENGAGED in learning by default.

As Cormier suggests, however, it's an open question as to whether engaged learning was ever the focus of schools to begin with. It's arguable that we've always wanted knowers over learners; just look at our assessments. But the fact that even those students who end up going to college are not engaged learners should trouble all of us greatly.

We should all be asking what causes students to lose their zeal for learning . . . *in school*. I believe every child carries that zeal to learn with him or her from the moment he or she is born. Think of those four-year-olds on the playground again. They're not just playing; they're constructing, testing hypotheses, seeing what works and what doesn't work, and learning powerfully in the process. They live to learn. And I'm convinced that kids don't lose their love of learning in general just because they get older. Even the most disengaged kids in the classroom go home and have a passion to learn a great deal without us. For example, while many adults may not see it as real learning, think about how much kids (and grown-ups) are constantly learning as they play the online video games that have become so pervasive. And it's more than just how to win the game; it's persistence, teamwork, collaboration, and much more.

So what happens in the school setting? Could it be the kids lose their passion to learn because we take away their freedom to learn? Because we begin to script and organize and plan almost every aspect of what they "learn" in school? While that's not the sole reason, I think it's a big part of it. In large measure, I've watched that happen with my own kids. (I can't forget my son's first-grade teacher beginning her back-to-school-night presentation with the words "First grade is where we learn the rules." Ugh.) If we really wanted engaged students, we'd let them organize their own learning pursuits, just as they do outside school, and we'd focus our efforts on helping them become literate, passionate learners and creators, not compliant sheep who are waiting to be told what to learn, when to learn it, how to learn it, and whether or not they've learned it.

Low Retention

A second indicator that the current schooling system is not working is the amount of "learning" that is quickly forgotten in schools. And again, this is something we all know. Try these five questions that just about every one of us answered correctly at some point in high school.

1. What are the three types of muscle tissue in the human body?

2. What is the most abundant element in the universe?

3. What is the circumference of a circle with a radius of 4?

4. In the sentence "The swimming pool is closed today," is the word *swimming* a participle or a gerund?

5. What is a hypotenuse?

In case you're wondering, the answers are (1) Smooth, skeletal, and cardiac; (2) Hydrogen; (3) 25.13; (4) Participle; and (5) The side opposite the right angle in a right-angled triangle.

If you knew the correct answers to all five of those, more power to you. As a former English teacher, I got the fourth one right. The other four? Not so much. But regardless of how many you got right, I wonder how often you've ever used any of this information outside of school.

Now multiply those types of questions by ten thousand, and you've got probably 90 percent of the curriculum we were tested on in school, 95 percent of which we've all forgotten. If we're honest about it, we know that much of what we teach our students in our classrooms will be forgotten shortly after they leave us. Save the basic literacies and numeracies that are required for all of us to communicate and function in the modern world, what did you learn in your first twelve years of education that matters in your life today?

That's a question that Harvard professor and author David Perkins (2014) asks in his book *Future Wise*. And he has a great reminder for us all: "It's nice to know a lot. But remember, knowledge not used is simply forgotten" (Perkins, 2014, p. 17). Yet the current emphasis in schools is on knowing, not learning—and not just on knowing in general but on knowing a fairly standard or common curriculum that, we have to remember, is just our current best guess as to what students need to have in their heads to be successful in their lives. And that guess hasn't changed much since 1892, when the Committee of Ten middle-aged white men convened to decide what every student needed to learn in high school. But seriously, is it even possible today to predetermine what is to be learned by every child? I think you know my answer.

We all know that the learning that sticks with us—in other words, the stuff that is truly learned—is the stuff that we actually use or apply in some important way in our lives. As Roger Schank (2011), another author in this series, once wrote, "There are subjects that are school subjects and there are subjects that are life subjects, and teenagers can tell the difference. They work harder at the life subjects" (p. 4). Or, to put it another way, "Dating is way more important than algebra and every teenager knows it" (Schank, 2011, p. 6). You probably know this too. Ask yourself this: What lessons learned do kids subsequently forget about dating or driving? I can tell you from watching my own kids the answer is veritably nothing.

For whatever reason, we adults seem not to want to acknowledge the fact that most of what students "learn" in school is quickly forgotten despite the fact that we ourselves never truly learned all that stuff either. We hang on to the myth that all these subjects and all this curriculum are crucial to every child's success in life even though we know from our own experience that that's simply not true. Author Daniel Quinn (2000) puts it this way:

> But there's another reason why people abhor the idea of children learning what they want to learn when they want to learn it. They won't all learn the same things! Some of them will never learn to analyze a poem! Some of them will never learn to parse a sentence or write a theme! Some of them will never read Julius Caesar! Some will never learn geometry! Some will never dissect a frog! Some will never learn how a bill passes Congress! Well, of course, this is too horrible to imagine. It doesn't matter that 90% of these students will never read another poem or another play by Shakespeare in their lives. It doesn't matter that 90% of them will never have occasion to parse another sentence or write another theme in their lives. It doesn't matter that 90% retain no functional knowledge of the geometry or algebra they studied. It doesn't matter that 90% never have any use for whatever knowledge they were supposed to gain from dissecting a frog. It doesn't matter that 90% graduate without having the vaguest idea how a bill passes Congress. All that matters is that they've gone through it! The people who are horrified by the idea of children learning what they want to learn when they want to learn it have not

accepted the very elementary psychological fact that
people (all people, of every age) remember the things
that are important to them—the things they need to
know—and forget the rest.

This is hard to argue against.

Outdated Definition of Success

The final indicator that the current school model isn't working as advertised is that our traditional measures of success aren't
being realized. This goes for higher education as well as K–12. The
explicitly stated goal of education is to make every student ready
for college or career, and while that's still a noble goal, we're not
achieving it.

Of the four million kids in the United States who enter high
school each year, only about 20 percent will have completed a two-
or four-year college degree eight years later (Halpern, Heckman, &
Larson, 2013). And of those who did earn a degree in 2012, only
about half were working in jobs that required a four-year college
degree (Mandel, 2014). That turns out to be about a 10 percent
"success" rate. While some of that is due to the economic problems
experienced from 2008 to 2013, much of it is also due to a fast-
changing job market and fundamental shifts in the workforce and
the skills, literacies, and dispositions now required to be a part of it.
Add to that the fact that students are carrying around more than $1
trillion in loan debt, and the picture gets even more dour.

Even more worrisome is that in a recent survey of CEOs done by
Northeastern University, fully 87 percent of them said that "most
college graduates lack the skills critical to success" (Ombelets, 2014).
If you don't believe that one, Gallup did a similar survey that found
only 11 percent of business leaders in America strongly agreed that
"graduates have the necessary skills and competencies to succeed in
the workplace" (Grasgreen, 2014). Not sure about you, but all of
that gives me pause when thinking about sending my own children

to university. (And that doesn't even take into account that the average college grad owes almost $40,000 in college debt when he or she leaves school [Samuelson, 2012].)

A Different Definition of Success

Given all of that—the lack of engagement, the focus on knowledge that is soon forgotten, the low level of success via college, and an already large and growing skills gap for success in the workplace—isn't it time that we consider that schools may be increasingly out of step with the realities of the modern learning world and that our current narratives and assessments grow more out of touch by the day? Isn't it time to consider a different definition of success?

No question, as I said before, rewriting the age-old narratives of schooling is not easy. In fact, I'm betting most of you reading this are in schools that have been labeled "successful" for years, if not decades, and that the focus of your work has continually been to become incrementally better at what you do, as measured primarily by local and state assessments, SAT scores, AP scores, and the like. Why should you change? It's a valid question that every school should be asking.

Well, here's my answer, at least: because now, finally, the changes that we see so prevalent in the real world are catching up to us. We can't ignore any longer that content and teachers and technologies are everywhere. Even more, we can't deny the amazing new opportunities for learning that technologies now bring us, opportunities that look nothing like what was possible in our learning lives when we were growing up. Opportunities that are built upon the freedom that access brings us to connect to information and people as we need or want them. Opportunities, importantly, that also are little understood by most educators, board members, and decision makers. I'm not blaming anyone here; these changes have come fast and big. But if you can make a compelling argument as to why we should wait any longer to reconsider our roles through these new contexts, I'd love to hear it.

Here's how Harvard professor and author Richard Elmore (2015) recently put it:

> While learning has largely escaped the boundaries of institutionalized schooling, educational reformers have for the past thirty years or so deliberately and systematically engaged in public policy choices that make schools less and less capable of responding to the movement of learning into society at large.
>
> Standards and expectations have become more and more literal and highly prescriptive in an age where human beings will be exercising more and more choice over what and how they will learn.
>
> Testing and assessment practices have become more and more conventional and narrow as the range of competencies required to negotiate digital culture has become more complex and highly variegated. . . .
>
> We are continuing to invest massively in hard-boundary physical structures in an age where learning is moving into mobile, flexible, and networked relationships. In other words, it would be hard to imagine an institutional structure for learning that is less suited for the future than the heavily institutionalized, hierarchical world that education reformers have constructed.

Or, as Weigel et al. (2009) argue:

> After millennia of considering education (learning and teaching) chiefly in one way, we may well have reached a set of tipping points: Going forward, learning may be far more individualized, far more in the hands (and the minds) of the learner, and far more interactive than ever before. This constitutes a paradox: As the digital era progresses, learning may be at once more individual (contoured to a person's own style, proclivities, and interests) yet more social (involving networking, group work, the wisdom of crowds, etc.).

> How these seemingly contradictory directions are ad-
> dressed impacts the future complexion of learning.

And it also, no question, impacts the future complexion of schooling. As the evidence mounts that the traditional, stated purposes of
schools are no longer being fulfilled, that the structures and systems
that we've used to frame the whole schooling experience are increasingly ineffective in dealing with the needs of the modern world, at
what point will we take a collective step back and begin to fundamentally rethink the purpose and value of schools in our kids' lives?
At what point do we begin to fundamentally change the language
around schooling as well? As author Christel Hartkamp (2014)
writes in *Knowmad Society*:

> In principle, the word "schooling" has become syn-
> onymous with the word "education" in our minds.
> It is therefore very hard to imagine education as a
> place different from a situation where young people
> are divided into age groups, are told what to learn by
> a teacher, are tested for their knowledge with a pre-
> determined curriculum, and believe that "real" life
> starts after having passed the final exam. For the
> same reason, the word "teaching" has become synon-
> ymous for the word "learning," and the word "testing"
> has become commingled with "knowing." Therefore,
> it is hardly surprising that anybody is questioning the
> principles underlying our schools. We need to invent
> a new language. (Kindle location 1934)

Disassociating "school" from "education" or "testing" from "knowing" will take a great deal of time, no doubt. But even more work
will be required for deconstructing some of the ways we think about
school systems in general.

System Structure

If we really step back and look at the educational system as it's
currently structured, it's hard to make a compelling case that we're
doing the best we can to support students as learners. When it

comes to much of the school experience, we take the path of least resistance, mostly because that's the way we've always done it. Let's look at some of these structures individually and compare them to modern-day learning environments.

We group students by age because that's the most efficient way to do it. But we all know that children develop at their own pace, that the idea that all eight-year-olds are ready to learn the same thing on the same day is kind of ridiculous, and that not allowing them to learn with peers who are older than they are actually limits what happens in class. In fact, school is the only place and time in our lives where we learn with only people of our own age. That reality never even existed until schools were invented.

Or what about subjects? It's just easier to separate things out into mathematics and history and English and science than it is to make learning more like the real world, where all that stuff gets jumbled together depending on what we're learning and why we're learning it. I'm not saying that a lot of the stuff that's in those subject-area buckets isn't worth learning (though I would argue way too much of it isn't). But subjects in the way we currently think about them are a construct created solely for the purpose of schooling, not for the purpose of learning. Interestingly, as I write this comes the news that schools in Finland are moving away from a subject-based experience to what they call *phenomenon teaching* or teaching by topic (Garner, 2015). For more on that kind of approach, read Roger Schank's (in press) book in this series, *Make School Meaningful—And Fun!*

The daily schedule with its assortment of bells is another construct that makes little (or no) sense when thinking about the learning we do outside of school. Forty-five- (or eighty-) minute blocks make it much easier for teachers to plan what to teach and to make sure that students become well-trained at following a constantly repeating pattern akin to what they might need to follow in a (now obsolete) factory job.

And then there's my favorite: assessments. I've yet to hear anyone argue convincingly that large- or small-scale standardized assessments are the best way to see if a child has actually learned anything, that it wouldn't be better to see if a student could actually employ whatever he or she was being asked to learn to solve an actual problem or to create something meaningful and beautiful and impactful in the world. That, unfortunately, would require way too much time, money, and effort to make sustainable in the current system. Oh, and of course, it would be way too hard to turn that into hard "data" upon which we can make generalizations on how to "improve" our current practice.

There are others, but you get my drift. We put our kids through a whole bunch of experiences in school that don't in any way reflect the real world and that are in place almost solely because they make our lives easier.

So here's the inescapable conclusion that we in education are going to have to come to terms with sooner rather than later for the sake of our kids: this moment of amazing access to an abundance of knowledge, information, teachers, and technology *demands* that we give our students the license and agency to learn freely *with* us so they can become experts at doing that *without* us. The longer we continue down the path of controlling their learning using outdated and increasingly irrelevant structures and systems, the more children we'll be turning out into the world without those skills, literacies, and dispositions that they need to flourish in the world.

Chapter 2
Learners Versus Knowers

Imagine for a moment that you're back in the midst of your adolescence, and you're standing in the entranceway of the biggest library you've ever seen. It's filled with stacks of books and magazines and various papers that go on as far as the eye can see to the right, to the left, and back. Even when you look up, you can't see the highest floor of this library; it looks like it must touch the clouds. It fills you with a mix of awe and excitement, almost too much to take in. But you can't wait to start digging through the shelves for everything you can find about World War II fighter planes or how to take better photos or that new musical group you've been listening to or whatever else you may have a passion to learn about.

Just as you step in to start taking a look around, however, you're stopped by a middle-aged man in a sport coat and tie who asks you how old you are.

"Thirteen," you say quietly, since you are in a library, after all.

"I see," the man says as he walks behind a large oak desk, opens a drawer, and starts to dig around in it. "Just one second . . . ah . . . here we go." He hands you a little, black, remote-like box and asks for your name, which he notes on a clipboard.

"What is this?" you ask.

"Why, it's your access key, of course," he says.

"Access key?" You frown as you turn it over in your hand. "What's an access key?"

"Just take the elevator up to the fifty-seventh floor, turn right, and follow the signs to the eighth-grade section," he says. "This key will let you in. I think there's four or five shelves full of materials up there now."

"Four or five shelves? But what about all this other stuff?" you ask as you sweep your arm across the vastness of the space. "You mean I can't look at any of it?"

"Oh no," he says. "You can't just roam around in here. We've already got everything you need to know picked out, and that's all that key will open. Now run along."

How do you think your thirteen-year-old self would feel at that moment? If you're like me, my guess is not real great. Frustrated. Mad, even. And yet, this is pretty much what we do to our connected kids every single day when they arrive in our classrooms. We tell them to put their amazingly huge online libraries away and focus only on the comparatively tiny slice of content and skills that we've preselected for them, just the stuff that we can fit into our one-thousand-hour-a-year curriculum, and we expect them to be OK with that. But they clearly are not. Remember, only 40 percent of high schoolers are engaged in school.

It's not just content that we keep from them but people, too. Imagine that same library populated by three billion people (who are now accessible online), many of whom could turn out to be amazing teachers and collaborators around the things you have a passion for. (Frankly, I don't know what I would do today in my personal [and professional] learning life without access to those people.)

And, of course, the same could be said of the technologies that now define our access—our laptops, tablets, and mobile phones—and the vast array of software, apps, and games that allow us to learn in ways few of us could imagine just a decade ago. I'm pretty sure I would be unable to create and connect and subsequently learn very effectively at all with the tool set that most schools limit their students to.

Access

Here we now are, in an amazing moment when the vast majority of our students are able to connect to nearly the sum of human knowledge, almost half the earth's population, and a powerful slate of tools. And what do we do? We limit their access to all of it in the service of a fairly traditional bucket of curriculum we have chosen through guesswork (which Seymour Papert rightly points out equals about one-billionth of 1 percent of the knowledge in the universe) (Stager, n.d.). And we also limit them to only the teachers we provide in their physical classrooms. Again, I'm not saying that those local classroom teachers aren't a valuable and important addition to our kids' learning lives. They are, and I want my own kids to be in classrooms with adults who will inspire and motivate them and care for them as human beings. But why would we deny a connection to other great teachers who are now accessible in the world?

Here's the larger, seminal question, however: Given the reality of this new library and the people and the tools, *what do we want our kids to know?* Do we really just want them to have (somewhat) mastered what's on those few shelves on the fifty-seventh floor, the stuff we've picked out and organized for them? The stuff that, like we ourselves already have, they're likely to forget? Or do we want them to know how to make sense of the abundance of that library, all that stuff and all those people and tools they now have at their fingertips to learn whatever they need to learn, whenever they need to learn it, with whoever can help them learn it? To put it another way, given the reality of access, *shouldn't the focus of our work now be to develop kids as learners instead of knowers?*

I'm not saying that there isn't a lot of crap in the library, that there aren't some not-so-nice people in the online population, or that there aren't a wide range of tools in the box that don't serve learning very well if at all. While the upside of access is powerful and amazing, unfortunately, it's not perfect. But it is the new reality that we have to figure out, and, importantly, that our kids have to figure out. Right now, with our laser-like focus on content, on the stuff that's easy to assess, and on using those assessments to evaluate and compare everything from teachers to schools to districts to nations, we're not doing much to help our kids develop as independent, persistent, literate learners. We're basically telling them to figure out what's crap and what isn't without us because anything that isn't in our curriculum isn't worth the bother. In essence, we're crossing our fingers and hoping for the best.

I'll say it again: our kids have a growing freedom to learn outside of school that is taken away every time they walk through a classroom door. The two experiences are increasingly at odds. They've always been at odds, really, when you compare the way children learn in school to the way adults learn after they have been through school. John Holt (1974), an author and an educator who is probably one of the greatest advocates for giving agency to children to learn, puts it this way:

> Young people should have the right to control and direct their own learning. . . . A person's freedom of learning is part of his freedom of thought, even more basic than his freedom of speech. If we take from someone his right to decide what he will be curious about, we destroy his freedom of thought. We say, in effect, you must think not about what interests and concerns you, but about what interests and concerns us. . . . As adults, we assume that we have the right to decide what does or does not interest us, what we will look into and what we will leave alone. We take this

right for granted, cannot imagine that it might be taken
away from us. (p. 240)

Yet we're seemingly OK with taking it away from kids once they
reach school age.

Choice

So let me ask you, given the choice between a learning environment in which someone or something tells you what you should be
interested in and concerned about and one where you have the freedom to pursue what you find interesting or important, which would
you choose? Given the choice between having access to one-billionth
of 1 percent of everything there is to know and having access to
the sum of human knowledge and information, which would *you*
choose? Given the choice between learning only from the people
you see in your face-to-face world and learning and creating and col-
laborating with scientists and authors and other passionate learners
from all around the world who want to learn more about the same
things you do, which would *you* choose?

I suspect that the vast majority of you reading this would choose
freedom and abundance over control and scarcity any day of the
week. I know I would. So why wouldn't we choose that for our
children as well? Do we really think that without the experience
of school in its current iteration there would be little or no chance
of them ending up successful and fulfilled as adults? Millions of
successful and fulfilled homeschooled adults would beg to differ.
School is by no means the only path; it's just the most well-worn
and, if we are honest about it, the most convenient path for most
parents. Do we limit this freedom because we think that we know
best when it comes to what all our kids should learn? I think we can
agree that we want all kids to be literate readers and writers, to know
enough mathematics and science to help them navigate the world
effectively, to have a sense of history, and so on. But now when we

and our kids have so much access to information and knowledge and the rest, what's more important—teaching our kids science and history and statistics or helping them develop the skills, literacies, and dispositions to interact with the world as scientists, historians, and statisticians who can use all these resources persistently and powerfully?

Let's not forget that when it comes to learning, freedom is the natural state of affairs before we go to school. Even before we can crawl, we are in a constant state of investigation and experimentation all in the service of learning. We have no "curriculum" for any of it. Our parents, with any luck, allow and nurture this exploration. Within some parameters built around keeping us safe, we're pretty much free to learn in whatever way works. Learning to walk is a process of trial and error. Learning to talk isn't an event, and our progress occurs without any plan or assessment. Consider that by six years old, children have a vocabulary that surpasses ten thousand words. That means that kids on average learn five new words a day, every day of their lives to that point—almost two thousand words a year without any real organization or design on the part of an adult. And, by the way, they forget almost none of it (Smith, 1998).

But even more, giving kids a freedom to learn in school makes them more successful in all parts of their lives. In classrooms where students are given the ability to choose their own topics for study and the methods and the people to study them with, the gains are huge. Reading, writing, and mathematics skills improve, and according to Professor Jennifer Keys Adair (2015) from the University of Texas, "Children show a vastly improved ability to absorb knowledge when they are allowed to make some of their own decisions about what they want to learn."

Other research has shown, not surprisingly, that freedom equals engagement in school. Writing in *TIME* magazine, DePaul University education professor Hilary Conklin (2015) concludes

that there is a compelling case to be made for play at every level of
the K–12 system:

> Giving students occasions to learn through play not
> only fosters creative thinking, problem solving, inde-
> pendence, and perseverance, but also addresses
> teenagers' developmental needs for greater indepen-
> dence and ownership in their learning, opportunities
> for physical activity and creative expression, and the
> ability to demonstrate competence. When classroom
> activities allow students to make choices relevant to
> their interests, direct their own learning, engage their
> imaginations, experiment with adult roles, and play
> physically, research shows that students become
> more motivated and interested, and they enjoy more
> positive school experiences.

Similarly, after almost a decade of research on the relationship
between curiosity and learning, Susan Engel (2015), the director of
Williams College's Program in Teaching, found that children who
are allowed to pursue their own questions reach higher levels of
intellectual achievement:

> People who are curious learn more than people who
> are not, and people learn more when they are curi-
> ous than when they are not. The fact that these two
> statements are different, and both true, makes it even
> more important to figure out what prevents schools
> from encouraging curiosity and what we might do
> about it. (p. 3)

Almost all the research shows that if you want kids to develop as
literate, articulate, persistent, curious, creative learners, freedom is
an absolute requirement.

Now, I know that many people who have the traditional school
experience develop all these qualities and more. There's no question
that for many students, the current system "works." But given the
realities of the traditional system compared to the realities of the
modern world of learning, I think it's arguable that moving forward
(and, actually, looking backward), people who carry those qualities

into their later lives will do so *despite* school, not because of it. Unless, of course, things change.

And here's the good news: things have started to change. Not with great speed, I'll admit. But more and more, I'm seeing deeper, more relevant conversations around change in schools that embrace the new freedoms and opportunities for learning that technology brings and, in some cases, more than just talk. Despite the difficulties, change can happen, both at the classroom and school levels.

Freedom to Change

If you've gotten this far, you've probably felt a niggling question just under the surface of this whole discussion. (For many, it may actually be on the surface.) It's one that I struggle with mightily, and in the end, it's probably the most important question of all: Can traditional schools and the systems and structures that support them evolve to the point where allowing students to learn freely using the abundant access to knowledge, information, teachers, and technologies becomes a feature and not a bug? Is it possible to take a school that's been operating under an industrial mindset for fifty or more years and turn it into a place where the emphasis truly becomes developing kids as learners instead of knowers?

To be honest, I'm not sure. Our narratives of the ways in which schools must operate are so hardwired that it's almost impossible to think of any real alternative. That's not to say there haven't been schools that have embraced freedom to learn as the fundamental premise of their work to educate kids even before the latest technological developments. But they haven't met with widespread affirmation. Take the idea (not to mention the practice) of the Sudbury schools, which evolved from the famous Summerhill School in England. These "free" (as in democratic, not cost) schools are held about as far to the "free" end of the school structure continuum as you can get. Seriously, most people actually chuckle or roll their eyes when I mention them in conversation or a presentation. Yet few would strenuously argue with statements such as "Sudbury schools believe that children have a natural desire to learn and to teach themselves" (Tallgrass Sudbury School, n.d.) or:

> When kids are free to manage their time and education they develop confidence, independence, responsibility, and resourcefulness. These qualities are important for life and will serve students well after school, making it easier for them to obtain further knowledge and achieve goals. (Tallgrass Sudbury School, n.d.)

Or:

> The fundamental premises of the school are simple—that all people are curious by nature; that the most efficient, long-lasting, and profound learning takes place when started and pursued by the learner; that all people are creative if they are allowed to develop their unique talents; that age-mixing among students promotes growth in all members of the group; and that freedom is essential to the development of personal responsibility. (Tallgrass Sudbury School, n.d.)

Most reasonable, caring educators who are learners in their own right would use much of this same language to describe their *personal* learning practice. I know I would. Where we struggle is when we get to what this might actually look like in school. For example:

> In a Sudbury school kids create their own curriculum and are free to spend their time however they choose . . . The Sudbury model does not have strict roles for students and teachers. Every member of the school is both a student and a teacher at any given time . . . The role of staff members is to mentor and help students seek resources, not to be an authority figure and tell students what to do or not do. (Tallgrass Sudbury School, n.d.)

That would just be chaos, right? In the context of the highly regulated, controlled, standardized narrative of the traditional system, it's no wonder Sudbury schools haven't gained a lot of traction.

But it's not chaos. Mark McCaig, who started a Sudbury school called Fairhaven School with his wife in 1998, says that "the school aims 'to strike that balance between freedom and responsibility'" (as cited in Vangelova, 2014). Kids are learning, pursuing their interests. To graduate, each student presents a culminating project that shows "that they have 'prepared themselves to become effective adults in the larger community'" (Vangelova, 2014). There *are* rules, but the difference is that the kids are the ones who have developed the rules, with the adults. And kids in Sudbury schools are by and large "successful" by traditional measures, as in the vast majority go on to college and do well in their careers (Sappir, 2009). However, the drastically different philosophies when it comes to structures and the way learning is thought of make most mainstream educators see Sudbury and other free schools as fringe alternatives. They just don't fit the narrative.

That's not to say, however, that the idea of giving students more freedom over their own learning only occurs in schools outside the mainstream. Educator Ira Socol (2009) has written extensively about his time in the 3Is (inquiry, involvement, and independent study) school in New Rochelle, New York, back in the early 1970s, a school built on the ideas:

> (1) that learning takes place best not when conceived as a preparation for life but when it occurs in the context of actually living, (2) that each learner ultimately must organize his own learning in his own way, (3) that "problems" and personal interests rather than "subjects" are a more realistic structure by which to organize learning experiences, (4) that students are capable of directly and authentically participating in the intellectual and social life of their community, (5) that they should do so, and (6) that the community badly needs them. (Postman, 1969)

According to Socol, all the trappings of the traditional system were dismantled. There were no grades, no required classes, no age groupings, and no "failures." He writes, "The school changed 'everything,' and in doing so liberated us to learn. Stripped away our excuses. And turned us loose to make the world our classroom" (Socol, 2009). But even more, there was a powerful culture established in the 3Is school that trusted children to learn on their own. Socol (2009) explains:

> [First,] students began each day knowing they had some level of control, they had put themselves into their situation. Second, [the school had] a real belief in students. No 3I teacher ever looked at a student and saw "failure." They might have seen problems, but they also saw opportunities. Third, [the school had] a belief in the power of adolescence. These adults knew kids would screw up, but they also knew that failure is how people learn—and that teenagers want to learn. So they dropped the cost of failure to almost zero. And people tried just about everything. Sometimes it worked, sometimes it didn't. But things were always learned along the way. Fourth, they embraced universal design before the idea had been described. "Do it the way that works for you," was the idea.

And how did that work out? As Socol writes, by traditional measures, very successfully. The graduation rate was 99 percent. Most kids went to four-year colleges, including some of the "best" schools on anyone's list. They turned out to be lawyers, scientists, teachers, diplomats, and more. In other words, the kids were all right. Ultimately, however, the school was not. It lasted for about fifteen years before succumbing to "conservative trends in education and budget cutting" (Socol, 2009). Again, the traditional narrative won out.

In more recent times, I've had the good fortune of visiting a lot of schools where students are asking their own questions, pursuing their own interests, and engaging in the process at a deep level. Among the most notable are the High Tech High fleet of schools in San Diego and the Science Leadership Academy in Philadelphia. While not totally free to learn, students there have a great deal more agency to self-select within a particular course what interests them and what they want to pursue. But those schools and most others of their ilk have been built for that purpose as opposed to having to overcome the obstacles of an ingrained old way of doing things in a district that has existed for decades. And I've been in lots of classrooms where teachers have created the conditions for students to exert agency and autonomy over the learning process. But too often those students graduate to classrooms where neither that agency nor autonomy exists.

And then there is the relatively new "Genius Hour" approach that many schools are using where students get at least some time during the week to pursue passion projects or learn about things of their own choosing. For some teachers and schools, it's a starting point for moving more agency and autonomy into the learners' hands. In some cases, like in educator and author A. J. Juliani's (2015) case, that amounts to 20 percent of a student's work in class, similar to the "20% time" that Google gives its employees to work on things that interest them. (That's how Gmail and Google Earth were born [Tate, 2013].) Juliani makes an interesting connection between the Google learning approach and the Montessori Method as developed by Maria Montessori at the start of the 20th century. Both support learning based on interests, emphasize hands-on work, allow for a freedom to explore, and are self-paced (Juliani, 2015).

More and more schools seem to be finding ways to implement similar passion-based learning experiences into their regular routines. If you want some examples, there's probably no better place than teacher Joy Kirr's LiveBinder site at http://bit.ly/ftlgh. All are predicated on the idea that we have to find ways to move more of the ownership of learning to the student, especially in these modern times. To be clear, many students initially struggle with the idea of having even a relatively small portion of their educational experience fully under their own control. As Juliani (2015) writes, when he introduced the concept to his students:

> Many were confused at first. Many were also excit-
> ed. Most did not know what to do with their free time.
> What I saw were students struggling to find a purpose
> for their own learning, when the purpose had always
> been provided for them. (p. xviii)

Eventually, most of his students ran with the freedom they were being given, and the reports back from most teachers I've spoken with who are implementing 20 percent time or some variation tell of higher student engagement, higher-quality work, and better outcomes on traditional assessments. Shocking, I know.

There are entire schools as well that are trying to bridge the gap between traditional and modern learning. Some, like Templestowe College, a secondary school in Australia, are taking a measured approach. There, students choose what time they'd like to start the day, what courses they want to pursue, and what types of assessments they'd like to use to show what they have learned. There are no mandatory courses after year 7, and students study at whatever level "is appropriate for them" (Carter, 2015), effectively ending the division of grade levels. Principal Peter Hutton says all those changes have had a huge effect on the culture of the school, not just among students but among teachers as well.

"I'm yet to come across a kid who doesn't love the school; that's a pretty rare thing in this day and age," Hutton says in an interview. "They feel that it is their choice. That is why they feel empowered" (Carter, 2015). Once again, it's about allowing students to follow their passions and then supporting them in that along the way.

"Here they're allowed to follow their passions and interests and not just in a minor way," Hutton explains in another interview. "They have total control, albeit signed off by their parents, to pursue their passions" (Preiss, 2014).

The move toward expanding choice for students at Templestowe came out of a dissatisfaction with the ineffectiveness of the school experience for so many kids. Hutton says that traditional school works for about one-third of students, with another third who don't come close to reaching their potential in a system that organizes and assesses every part of the experience. But it's the last third, those for whom school is an abysmal experience, where the enhanced freedom really makes a difference. School has become about what these students want to learn (Carter, 2015). Enrollment numbers at the school are way up, students and parents are more satisfied with the learning experience, and teachers have taken a real liking to the opportunity to teach engaged students.

Beyond individual classrooms and schools, there is some good news at the national and provincial levels as well. In some parts of the world, the rhetoric around schooling is changing. Read British Columbia's Education Plan from 2012, and you can't help but feel hopeful:

> We need to put students at the centre of their own education. We need to make a better link between what kids learn at school and what they experience and learn in their everyday lives. We need to create new learning environments for students that allow them to discover, embrace, and fulfill their passions. We need to set the stage for parents, teachers, administrators and other partners to prepare our children for success not only in today's world, but in a world that few of us can yet imagine. (Abbott, n.d., p.2)

The government of Alberta (2014) similarly recognizes that:

> Today's students require a well-rounded education to prepare them for the future. We live in a world where anyone can discover the secrets of the Arctic without leaving the house, or peek at the depths of the ocean at the click of a mouse. Knowledge isn't limited to textbooks anymore. We're helping our students to understand new learning tools, inspiring them to become ethical citizens and engaged thinkers with an entrepreneurial spirit. The world is changing. And our approach to education needs to change with it.

Despite all of these movements in the direction of a more classic approach to learning in the classroom, rare are the instances where the level of transformation or change has been reached at 100 percent or even close.

Requirements for Change

Obviously, it's easier to speak of change than it is to enact real change in classrooms. Among other things, every school needs a visionary leader who not only understands the new contexts for learning but can motivate members of every constituency to engage in the hard conversations that are necessary. And that leader needs to be in it for the long haul, as change of the type I'm suggesting can't be done in just a few years. Public schools need school boards that support iteration and change, teachers unions that allow for innovation, and parents and community members who are comfortable with their kids having a school experience that differs from their own. In the long run, they need policymakers who will work to remove onerous assessment and accountability structures that currently impede the potential for real learning in classrooms, the type that isn't always easy to measure but is crucially important to develop nonetheless. And while they may differ on the edges, long-standing private schools have the same challenges, in addition to having to draw enough paying students each year to remain sustainable.

In short, a real, fundamental shift from a school-organized education to a self-organized education (with the help of school) takes a great deal of conviction, courage, and commitment. The conviction part is around the belief that schools in their current iteration don't support real learning in the ways our modern kids require. The courage piece is to actually stand up and say exactly that to a whole bunch of people who are fully invested in that current iteration of schools. Commitment is necessary because none of this will come quickly or easily. (With the average tenure of public school superintendents being just three years, this is especially problematic [Nott, 2015].)

Case Study: The Mosaic Collective

Do you think that at your school, 10 percent of the families of your students would be willing to opt into something radically different from the traditional system, something that rejects most of our "old school" thinking and offers up a truly bold way of functioning and considering student learning?

I've been asking that question to many of the educators I've met in my travels. Would it surprise you to hear that most quickly respond with a firm "yes"? It doesn't surprise me at all. I think there are enough deeply disaffected kids in all our schools that 10 percent wouldn't be a problem for most. And I'm not just talking about the kids who are struggling academically; I'm talking about "successful" kids, kids who are making the grade but not having an especially wonderful time doing it. Kids like Jeremy Dortch, the young man featured in this book's introduction. Jeremy's school, Castle View High School, is the only traditional school I know of that has attempted to rewrite the narrative of public schooling. That's not to say that the whole school of about 1,900 students is suddenly free to learn in the contexts we've been talking about here. But just more than one hundred of them are in a program they've called The Mosaic Collective (TMC), and the idea is to build that out to more and more students each year. The bio for the program explains:

> Born in 2014 out of experience, frustration, curiosity, and a sense of educational righteousness, The Mosaic Collective is a project-based, problem-based, inquiry-based, and challenge-based learning environment housed in a traditional public high school. All together, we are a student-based learning program that trades the bureaucratic distractions of the school factory and misguided over-reliance on content for the bliss of intrinsic learning and a strong focus on the needs of our students.
>
> As teachers in Mosaic we embrace our new roles. Our work is interdisciplinary, purposeful, and always

challenging. We employ methods of design thinking to continuously iterate and evolve our ideas and practices. We work with and alongside our students to build a true collective of learners.

The Mosaic Collective does not grade nor does it adhere to traditional bell schedules. It empowers, trusts, creates and contributes while honoring interests, passions, and dreams—of both students and teachers alike. (McClintock, 2015)

I want to emphasize the following line because I like it so much: "the bliss of intrinsic learning and a strong focus on the needs of our students." Learning is bliss when it's done to serve our personal goals rather than someone else's, isn't it? And all schools should be about the modern needs of their students. To me, those are the two things that make Mosaic so interesting.

That frustration noted in the Mosaic bio was felt most deeply by Castle View teachers Michael Schneider and Ryan McClintock, who, along with a handful of other teachers and Principal Jim Calhoun, asked for and received permission from the powers that be in their district to start the program. As it comes without bells, grades, subject areas, homework assignments, tests, or just about anything else mappable to the traditional system, the folks at Mosaic are doing a total re-envisioning that they believe fits more closely with the way real learning takes place. And that new vision of what learning in schools needs to be is based on some deep-seated beliefs about schooling developed from more than one hundred years of collective experience on the part of the founding teachers. Through this experience, they have come to know the following about most high school freshmen. They:

- Are not truly self-motivated to learn in a traditional academic setting. They need external rewards or punishment for motivation.
- Are not oriented toward long-term goals. Instead, school forces them to focus on short term successes or goals (test, week, project).

- Do not know what they are passionate about or lack the inspiration to pursue that passion within the traditional academic setting.
- Have limited awareness of their potential powerful relationship to the larger communities in which they reside. (Schneider, 2014)

The vision these educators are implementing is also based on a full realization of the "modern" contexts that are beginning to have such a huge impact on the way we learn and the concept of school. The program's website explains:

Catalyzed by developments in the broad field of technology, much of how we live and function is changing. Life is becoming evermore connected. Never has so much information been so readily and universally accessible. Social media and so-called Web 2.0 are essentially blurring time and erasing barriers. We seem to be available 24/7/365 for conversation, texting, instant messaging, and video conferencing. And yet the mammoth institution of public education remains largely unchanged. To "do well" in school often means students must detach from real-world problems and opportunities in order to learn isolated and seemingly useless bits of information. Many teachers continue to simply lecture content to students, which completely ignores the ever-increasing number of verbal and nonverbal signals our students continuously send us. They're practically begging us to stop and let them explore, discover, and connect in real, authentic, and meaningful ways. (CV Mosaic Collective, n.d.)

But, as noted earlier in this chapter, it takes courage. (Why we should need courage to move agency for learning to the learner is ironic, no?) I've visited Mosaic a number of times and had extensive conversations with Michael and Ryan and Jim and others. When I interviewed Jim for a podcast in 2014, he talked about not taking the easier route to change. "My passion is to create an environment and a public school that is addressing the needs of the future, not creating my own new school and a charter school environment where I just select the kids," he said. "I want this to work with any kid who walks in the building, not just a select group" (J. Calhoun, personal communication, October 30, 2014).

And after years of personal soul-searching about the effectiveness of traditional education, and months of conversations with Michael, Ryan, and others about their own frustrations, Jim decided to trust his fundamental beliefs about learning and push for the very different space that Mosaic represents.

"We need to start with where the kids are, what they're enthusiastic about, what they're interested and passionate about, because that's what drives them to deeper and deeper levels of learning," he said. "When you just assign somebody something to learn, they're either going to go through the motions or they're going to not do much with it at all, or in some cases revolt and not do anything."

No question, certain restrictions apply; this is still a public school in a state that has a large number of requirements to meet and assessments to pass. Yet Jim and his team are convinced that giving kids more freedom to pursue their interests can still square with those traditional outcomes and, in fact, go far beyond them in terms of the types of deep learning experiences kids need in order to flourish.

"What we're trying to do is have kids pick their own path and design a project or solve a problem that interests them," he said. "With the guidance of the teacher, they figure out which particular standards that their project is going to attack, and over the four years, they design their own curriculum to meet the graduation requirements."

So what does that look like in practice? It looks like Jeremy Dortch. Think about how many students you know who would say this: "I feel that I have complete control over my education. . . . I have the freedom to really explore what I am interested in, in what I really want to pursue for the rest of my life" (J. Dortch, personal communication, March 10, 2015).

Now, I know some cynics will say that, as a sophomore, Jeremy probably really doesn't know what he'll do with the rest of his life and that he needs the intervention of adults and systems to help him figure it out. No doubt, at fifteen years old, few kids have a clear and specific path forward to a career or lifelong passion. As we all know, that stuff changes. But that's the beauty of the Mosaic experience for Jeremy; he can change it. He's not restricted by the traditional structures that chain most students to a wide but not deep learning experience in school. Even though many of the adults in schools might disagree with his characterizations of traditional school, I think the way he articulates the differences between his current education and his old one is fascinating on a lot of levels:

> In regular school, students are educated for the sole purpose of answering questions on a test to demonstrate what they have learned. For the sake of scheduling, all students in traditional classes at my school must choose, at most, eight credits worth of classes to take for the next year. In Mosaic, I can take more than the eight class limit. I don't have to work on each class for exactly 85 minutes at a time. If need be, I can work all day on my chemistry project, or I can work on it in small 10 minute increments. I get to do what works best for me. In Mosaic, we demonstrate our learning by the mastery of concepts; we will not move on to the next step until we have demonstrated mastery of the first step. The freedom to choose my topics has led to a passion for that topic that would almost never be touched upon in regular school. This passion causes me to want to learn everything I can about my topic, I don't need to stop once I've done enough work to get an A, I can keep on learning. The restriction of a grade doesn't exist here. I don't work to meet the requirements that my teachers set; I work for myself. (J. Dortch, personal communication, March 10, 2015)

How many of our students might echo similar frustrations with traditional school? (I know my own kids do on a regular basis.)

As Jeremy says, he works for himself, but he also works for his classmates. What Jeremy chose to study early on in the Mosaic school was design, as in design (and redesign) of the classroom space that those first one hundred kids were sharing. Part of that meant learning how to read construction blueprints, capping off electrical outlets, creating floor plans and color schemes collaboratively with others, and a whole bunch more. So when the maintenance man asked how Jeremy had learned to cap off the outlet, the answer was that it was part of his personal curriculum around classroom design, specifically the Mosaic classroom. He learned it because it was a necessary step toward understanding and reaching his personal goal as a learner and creator and it was something he cared about.

And that's the key thing to remember. It wasn't so much the "how." It was the "why." Jeremy had an authentic interest in learning it based on an actual, real-life need. He was, as Dewey advocated, learning by doing. And to Jeremy, that makes all the difference in the world. He told me:

> In Mosaic, my education not only consists of the basic knowledge that all students are required to learn to graduate high school, but also important life skills such as how to send a well-worded email, when to dress professionally for a meeting, how to work in a group with several contrasting ideas, and how to listen to different opinions and then form my own. . . . Because of Mosaic, I think that I am a better critical thinker, I feel more challenged on a daily basis. (J. Dortch, personal communication, March 10, 2015)

When I tell the story of Mosaic to others, two questions are sure to arise. The first revolves around whether every student is self-motivated enough to flourish in an environment predicated on these types of freedoms. People will say things like "Not every kid is an autodidact, you know" or something similar. And I always respond with "Really? Ever see a five-year-old who *isn't* a self-motivated learner?"

While I touched on this earlier, I'll ask you the same question, and the one that naturally follows it: What happens to kids between the time they're five and fifteen? Could it be that the more structure and organization we create around learning, the more agency and autonomy we take away from kids as they go through the system, the more they lose their natural curiosity and desire to learn on their own? Honestly, I think that's a no-brainer.

But I'm not suggesting that even with the sometimes suffocating structures and regulations of schools that fifteen-year-olds still aren't self-motivated learners. I could tell you stories about my own teenagers learning (on their own) to play Minecraft or learning about becoming a vegan or learning to shoot a basketball like a professional or a whole bunch of other stuff that isn't in the typical high school curriculum. They're just not self-motivated to learn the stuff that we put in front of them in school because nine times out of ten it's about "how" and not any real "why" that is meaningful to their lives.

Yet in our role as educators, we carry on, organizing and structuring, tending to listen to the voice on what Papert (1993) terms the "school side" of our brains even when we know what's happening at Mosaic and Sudbury and in informal learning spaces online is much closer to the natural state of affairs. The idea of formal learning in a school is so ingrained in our experience and expectations and policies that everything else is seen as an outlier, an experiment, and not a viable alternative. It doesn't have to be this way, but as I said before, it takes conviction, courage, and commitment to make informal, self-directed student learning the norm in schools. The teachers at Mosaic, and to some extent the students as well, will tell you that it took a certain period of "detox" to shake loose of the constraints of the traditional system and finally feel comfortable with a freer learning environment. Monika Hardy (2010), another educator who has been working with free learning spaces, says that detox "is simply a process of learning to learn, of knowing what to do when you don't know what to do"—in other words, when someone isn't telling you what to do. That's not the emphasis in traditional schools, where we condition kids to sit and wait to be told what to learn, when to learn it, how to learn it, and how they'll be assessed on it. In essence, we need to give kids the time they need to get back to the state where their natural rhythms and motivations for learning take over.

The second question people always bring up is "Will the kids be OK?" as in, Will they get into college? Will they be able to create opportunities for themselves? Will they flourish in their own lives both professionally and personally? These questions are unanswerable for any child, whether in a traditional school setting or one like Mosaic. But to doubt Jeremy and his fellow students is also to doubt his teachers who know full well the myriad of definitions of "success" that people who are watching this new program are looking for. They know perfectly well the balance they need to strike between the traditional outcomes that are still in place and the highly nontraditional roles they need to play in classrooms where freedom, agency, and autonomy around learning are the mainstays and not just on the edges.

Chapter 3
The Freedom to Teach

If we are to transfer agency over the learning process to our students and create an environment and a culture in schools that support a greater freedom to learn, what exactly is the role of a teacher? Suffice it to say, I think there is a hugely important role for adults to play in schools moving forward. It's just a different one from the role they've played to date. Their role is no longer the subject-matter expert as much as it is the person who creates the conditions for kids to learn deeply and powerfully in the classroom. While we can't control a child's passions or interests (nor would we want to), we can control the extent to which those passions and interests flourish in his or her time with us, all of which tracks pretty closely to what those participants in the Big Ideas Global Summit in 2010 concluded.

Eliminating Obstacles

In thinking about the changing role of teachers at a moment when students have more opportunities to learn on their own, the participants of the summit felt that:

> Such learning requires counsel; it requires nurturing; it requires the wisdom and guidance of great teachers, who, from the time of Socrates and his learned Greek colleagues, have refined our notions of pedagogy until, in the forum of contemporary technologies, we are

now challenged to anchor our thinking back with the
learner. We must flip our perspective and ask how the
art and science of contemporary teaching and learning might now make it possible for us to be able to
reach, not just those few who made it to the Agora;
not just the privileged who were allowed to attend the
institutions of school over past centuries, but rather all
young people. To do this we need to shift our thinking
from a goal that focuses on the delivery of something—a primary education—to a goal that is about
empowering our young people to leverage their innate
and natural curiosity to learn whatever and whenever
they need to. The goal is about eliminating obstacles
to the exercise of this right—whether the obstacle is
the structure and scheduling of the school day, the
narrow divisions of subject, the arbitrary separation of
learners by age, or others—rather than supplying or
rearranging resources. The shift is extremely powerful.
(Dixon & Einhorn, 2011, p. 6)

I find that idea of eliminating obstacles to learning especially compelling. And that speaks directly to the work of the teachers at Mosaic,
the extent to which they are changing their own practice, how they,
in essence, are being given a freedom to teach in compelling new
ways for both themselves and their students. Teachers don't do lesson
plans, as there are no "lessons" per se. They respond to the individual
needs of students as they occur as opposed to teaching the same concepts and ideas to all kids on the same day in the hope that they'll
remember those concepts if and when they need them. Among the
Mosaic staff, you'll find expertise in almost every subject, and in
those that might be missing, the staff can connect kids to others
who can help them.

What I love about these teachers is that they didn't wait for the
system to change; they set about changing the system. It wasn't easy
to get Mosaic up and running, and it hasn't been a smooth path
through the first year. But they have been guided (and motivated) by
their belief that schools can be different, that students can be trusted
to do great things when given the opportunity to freely decide their

own learning paths, and that their greatest service as "teachers" is in the form of co-learners with their students. Here's how McClintock (2015) explains it:

> The freedoms to learn offered by our program know no bounds. They can extend well beyond traditional school hours, as students and teachers use social media and texting to share information, ideas, and questions. As a science teacher I love it when I can stretch my expertise and content into other areas like history, writing, world language, and math. It's just so natural to do this and in doing this I am exposed to new ideas. I learn so much in Mosaic.

The dissonance between the traditional experience and what has been created at Mosaic is acute. McClintock (2015) writes:

> When teachers see themselves first and foremost as master explainers they can front-load content to a point devoid of exploration and discovery. And desires to make things easy and understandable can come at the expense of students' making their own connections after wrestling with an idea or concept. In short, our good intentions may have created unhealthy, uninspired, and unnatural environments in which to learn enduring lessons and skills. We've over-thought ourselves into a hole so deep that others think we need rescue and reform. How many of these reforms are simplifying? How many of these reforms free teachers to create, inspire, and mentor?

> In Mosaic . . . we seek to do just these things. And I am finding my newfound freedoms so liberating and refreshing. I am not just a master explainer. . . . I am a free mind not bound by the artificial constraints of a burdened system lost in a maze of its own creation. I am free to learn with my students; I am free to teach and to be taught; and I am free to dream and make connections that extend well beyond the walls of school and the start and finish times of a traditional school day.

And it is also interesting the extent to which giving students the reins to their own learning changes the way we think about curriculum and our use of it to support student learning rather than to drive it. My friend Bruce Dixon (in press), another author in this series, describes this as a move away from curriculum as orthodoxy to, instead, strategy. Here's how McClintock (2015) thinks about it:

> As a teacher in Mosaic I am the consummate researcher. Teachers are researchers, but many fail to identify themselves in this manner. I have a front row seat to "ah-ha" light bulb moments, fatigued breakdowns, . . . I know my students well and so, too, they know me. I've never grown so close to a group of students in such a short period of time. The freedom to teach in Mosaic affords me the opportunities to . . . nimbly respond to their needs in ways that were not always possible in a traditional environment. I leave my school on a daily basis wondering about my students' threads of investigations—I hear songs and stories on the radio as I drive home that may be of interest to them, I watch videos and think of how they may overlap with the ideas shared with me by my students, I naturally find and share books, links, and relay aspects of conversations I have with colleagues, parents, neighbors, friends, and even complete strangers.

No question, the story of Mosaic is still nowhere near complete. While Jim and Ryan and Michael will tell you they are more than happy with what's transpired over the last year, they still have much to learn. In a school with no grades, how will kids get into college? (Hint: They will. Many schools, such as Poughkeepsie Day School (Poughkeepsie, New York), Eagle Rock School (Estes Park, Colorado), and the Waring School (Beverly, Massachusetts), don't give grades, and they send their students to university.) How will student athletes meet the NCAA standards for participation? (No answer yet.) And what about the state tests and other legacies of the traditional system that Mosaic students are going to have to deal with? As the principal, Jim Calhoun, will tell you, they're building it as they go. But none of them sees an obstacle too great to overcome that would make them turn back.

Barriers to Freedom

What strikes me more than anything about the Mosaic story is this: a group of educators had the courage to admit what they knew from their own personal lives, that deep and powerful learning happens most often when we are free to pursue our passions and interests in authentic and relevant ways, especially when doing so with others who share our passions, and that schools by and large suppress that. Unlike most in education, not only did they acknowledge that, they had the conviction to act on it.

So what then are the barriers that stop most of the rest of us from bringing more of a freedom to learn approach into our classrooms? And, more importantly, what, if anything, can we do about them?

That last part is crucial because, as much as I've spoken to educators around the world who are totally aware and in agreement as to what's required for kids to learn powerfully in their lives, all too often those same people feel powerless to change the conditions in their classrooms. And make no mistake, in many parts of the United States, the expectations and evaluations being put upon teachers are onerous; they are not in any way freeing in the sense that we've talked about here. I don't think anyone is shocked at recent news reports that say enrollments in teacher preservice programs are down in the United States (Westervelt, 2015), Australia (Bita, 2015), and elsewhere.

Put simply, the barriers are numerous. Fear of change, well-financed lobbyists driving policy, lack of leadership and clear vision, legacy systems and structures, ignorance around the changes that are occurring, parents' traditional expectations—all of these and more have been cited by the folks I've talked to about moving schools and classrooms to a more progressive, modern approach. Despite the obvious disconnect most of us feel between school and nonschool learning, change is terribly hard. Three of the toughest barriers that are most often brought up are (1) tradition and nostalgia, (2) assessment regimes, and (3) postsecondary requirements.

Tradition and Nostalgia

Without question, the biggest barrier to rethinking schooling in response to the changing worldscape is our own experience in schools. It's what we know, and as educators or parents, the familiar feels safe to us and for our kids. Intellectually, we may be able to make sense of the argument laid out in this book, that the world has changed, that being a learner is more important than being learned, and that for our kids to have the best chance of success in the world, they have to be able to flourish in freedom. In *DIY U* (as in "Do It Yourself University"), author Anya Kamenetz (2010) explores the many new potential paths to becoming educated in the abundantly connected world and interviews a number of parents who expressed just those sentiments but were unable to "sanction" any different type of school experience for their kids. Read the comments on any article about progressive ideas in education in the *New York Times* or elsewhere, and you get the sense that most are still in the business of doubling down on doing better on traditional outcomes rather than rethinking the whole concept.

To be brutally honest, I've struggled with this myself. In fact, looking back on it, given the chance to do it over with my own children, I'm pretty sure I would have done it much differently when it came to their schooling. Don't get me wrong—my kids weren't seriously harmed by school, and their teachers, for the most part, were good, caring people who were doing their best given the pressures of policy and parents and tradition. But it could have been so very much better than it was when it came to giving them an environment that honored their own learning and developed them as curious, creative, passionate learners in the world. I'll admit, on some level, to feeling a great deal of sadness about that. I've been asked on numerous occasions why we didn't pull our kids out of school or find more progressive schooling alternatives for them. I've been called a hypocrite, in fact. And I totally understand why.

It's no excuse, but my enlightenment around these issues came very late in my life. By the time I fully understood learning in both the traditional and modern sense, my kids were too entrenched in their social circles and activities to consider pulling them out. Instead, we've tried to "co-school" them, encourage them to pursue their passions and learning outside school, and limit the deleterious effects of standardization and control as much as possible. This has not been easy.

So how do educators move to help teachers and parents and community members to a place where they have modern convictions about schooling and the courage to advocate for them? In a word, we work to educate them. If we are convinced that learning environments that give students more agency and freedom over their own learning are what our students need and we are committed to bringing those environments into our schools, then we have to make that case to all members of the school community. I've seen superintendents do this by engaging in book studies with parent groups, sharing curated readings with them through newsletters and websites, and actively engaging community members in discussions about the future and our efforts to ready our kids for it.

Assessment Regimes

If a lack of a modern context among stakeholders isn't bad enough, the current assessment regimes that we employ are almost worse when it comes to standing in the way of serious change in classrooms. We are hyperfocused on the easy-to-measure parts of the school experience. Supposedly, they provide us actionable data and ways to compare our progress (or lack thereof) within our own schools and districts and with other schools. We can use the results to see if we are closing achievement gaps (while basically ignoring learning gaps). In addition, measuring the measurable makes it easy to tell if a teacher is doing a better or worse job compared to other teachers, but it does not factor in variables such as the socioeconomic status and preparedness of the students in their classrooms. And, finally, current standardized assessments are a multibillion-dollar industry—more than a quarter billion just for Pearson alone (Simon, 2015)—that few in the business (or in the statehouse) have any real interest in changing. (No one is shocked to hear that the four biggest firms in the testing business spend millions of dollars to lobby lawmakers at every level [Strauss, 2015], right?)

In short, the skills, literacies, and dispositions that are required for success in today's quickly changing world are not easy to measure and, therefore, are not seen as priorities. Sure, we talk about curiosity and creativity and persistence and flexibility (and more) as being crucial for all learners in a more self-organized, abundant world. But assessing those attributes cannot be standardized and would therefore require more time and expense than most are willing to pay. So instead of assessing the things we value, we end up valuing the things we assess, which ends up being just about anything that's easy to measure.

Removing this barrier is not easy and requires, again, a great deal of education for community members and policymakers. While we should all be active in our efforts to vote out lawmakers who know little about education and who only want to do "better" as evidenced by test scores, we can't wait for regime change to occur. Instead, we need to begin to create more performance- and reflection-based assessments for the classroom level that are transparent in the sense that parents and others can see evidence of growth in their child's ability to learn, not just in their child's ability to get the right answer.

Postsecondary Requirements

It's the perception of many in education that, if kids are given more freedom to learn around the things they find interesting or relevant, they won't be college ready, that they will have missed certain courses or buckets of information that are required to be accepted into university. Educational leaders at traditional schools are loathe to mess with the recipe, so to speak, especially in systems where the vast majority of students do go on to college. Yet, as you read this, many books are being written and published about the future of higher education, the different paths that are emerging, and the growing expectation that, over the next decade or so, the whole story of higher education (excluding the highly prestigious institutions that have huge endowments and more applicants than they know what to do with) will begin to be rewritten. And, not surprisingly, that new narrative will include a lot more freedom for students to choose their own paths to the mastery and expertise that used to be the provenance of the university.

It may feel like a big risk to deviate from the proverbial script, but let's remember that in the United States, only about one-third of the population ends up with a four-year college degree. And for the average college graduate, that means entering the world with a good chunk of debt and, as I suggested earlier, about a 50 percent chance of getting a job that actually uses the degree that he or she earned. That doesn't make a great argument for sticking to the script.

No one is suggesting (yet) that our kids shouldn't aspire to higher education. But we do have to understand what a "higher education" means right now and what it might mean for tomorrow. I know I sound like a broken record, but once again, this requires a re-education of everyone involved in the conversation around schooling and learning. And it means being comfortable with acknowledging the paths to adulthood that don't include college right out of high school. Online and offline apprenticeships, self-organized learning opportunities, and doing real work regardless of the level of "education" are all a part of that even though they look and feel "different." Just one example of the ways in which it's clear that most are not yet comfortable with this concept is the shock I witness when people ask where my daughter, the high school senior, is going to college next year and I tell them she's not because she's taking some time off to figure out what she wants to do with her life.

I'm not naive enough to suggest that we can just sweep these barriers (and the others) away by saying, "The world has changed, and we have to do things differently." As I've said, these narratives run deep. But on some level, that's exactly what we're going to have to do. It's not just our kids whom we need to educate; it's all those other folks who are a part of the larger school conversation. And while we each play a role in that, I will tell you that it's a lot easier to make some headway with a visionary, committed leader who is in for the long haul. The schools and districts that are moving the furthest fastest have those types of leaders. It requires re-creating the mission and vision for what an education looks like, and it requires pushing back against the status quo in thoughtful, measured ways (including the book studies, newsletters, and so on mentioned earlier). It's not easy, but the good news is more and more are beginning to understand the opportunities and challenges of the moment and move their schools and districts forward.

Epilogue:
The End of the Beginning

Schools should teach everything that anyone is interested in learning.

—John Dewey

When Dewey said this one hundred or so years ago, I'm sure most scoffed at the idea. "How would we do that?" they might have asked, with good reason, or even, "*Why* would we do that?" Back then, most saw education not as an individual pursuit but as a collective experience that we fashioned for our kids, preparing them for an industrial economy where much of the world was driven by standardization and manufacturing and following rules. The idea that a child's interests would drive his or her education was not the prevailing attitude. Many would have thought it silly, in fact.

Despite the vast changes that have occurred since Dewey's time, especially changes in the last decade or so, that attitude remains. It's as if the idea of school is immune to revision if not reinvention. Even though Dewey's mission could be realized today given all that we have access to in this moment, we rarely entertain or articulate anything close to that when it comes to the ways we think about students learning in our schools.

But the bigger frustration is this: even though a growing number of educators know that we *could* now move our classrooms and systems to a more learner-centered, interest-based experience, I really believe most of us know that we *should* have been working toward that all along. For we are not just educators; we are learners, and as such, we know some undeniable truths about learning and schooling.

- We know that deep and powerful learning requires a personal interest in whatever is being learned.

- We know that deep and powerful learning is not served by constraining time, separating out subjects, or limiting our exposure to others of a different age or experience.

- We know that much of what kids "learn" in school is soon forgotten.

- We know that kids' deep and powerful learning outside the classroom looks nothing like what happens in the classroom.

- We know that children who learn in other nonschool environments end up just as well prepared for life if not more so than children in traditional systems.

- We know that grades and assessments define our kids in ways that are counterproductive if not harmful.

- We know that not all children learn the same thing in the same way on the same day.

We know all of this because these are all truths in our own personal learning lives. Yet we continue to act in schools as if we know little or any of it.

The reasons why we do this are complex, but I'm not sure they matter that much any longer. The fact is that learning is leaving the building. Our kids are swimming in seas of access where they are able to learn deeply without us. And if we don't begin to shift our focus in schools from control and organization to freedom and self-direction, we're going to suffer some deep consequences as a society and as a world. With all the fast-growing and changing complexities of life on Earth staring us in the face, I'm betting on the learners to see us through, not those who are waiting for someone else to script their learning for them.

As I've said, this will not be easy. But it's worth the effort. As education writer Kris Shaffer (2015) says:

> If we want education to transform the way our students see the world, we must set aside the safe, but flawed, thinking of curriculum as content—pedagogy as the careful, logical ordering of facts through which we lead our students. Transformative education is dangerous. It allows teachers, and students, the freedom to fail . . . and the freedom to be brilliant. This is education. Not the universal meeting of a preset standard, nor the study of the brilliance of dead celebrities. Rather, education is the empowering of students to push against the standards, to discover and cultivate their own brilliance. To learn what it means to be free.

Or, as author Christel Hartkamp (2014) writes:

> A new era has begun, and, more than ever there is a demand for innovative, creative thinkers. Society needs people that can adapt to a fast-changing world, in which we do not yet know what kind of skills will be needed to be successful in the future. The only way to educate our kids is by letting them experiment with uncertainty. (Kindle location 2178)

Even so, we have to realize that giving students freedom and the uncertainty that goes with it is not enough. Our work moving forward must be centered on helping students develop literacy and fluency in the freedom to learn. We don't just have to change the narrative when it comes to schooling; we have to change the culture as well. That requires a deep appreciation on our part for the opportunities and challenges that this moment of access brings. It requires that we exercise our own freedom to learn in these new ways so we can best prepare our students to take full advantage of them as well.

But in the end, all of this is dependent on your own personal decisions around what to do moving forward. If I've convinced you that the world has changed, that the outcomes and expectations we have for kids have changed, and that the true transformation in schools revolves around enhancing freedom and autonomy and agency for the learners in our charge, then what will you do? What level of conviction do you have in the need for that type of change? How committed are you to bringing those changes about? And how much courage do you have to lead the way instead of wait for a better or easier moment down the road?

References and Resources

Abbott, G. (n.d.). *BC's education plan*. Victoria, British Columbia, Canada: British Columbia Ministry of Education. Accessed at www.bcedplan.ca/assets/pdf/bc_edu_plan.pdf on April 5, 2015.

Adair, J. K. (2015). *In test-based systems, even young kids resist learning*. Accessed at www.childcarecanada.org/documents/research-policy -practice/15/03/test-based-systems-even-young-kids-resist-learning on April 6, 2015.

Bita, N. (2015, March 20). 'Daggy' tag turning school leavers off teaching as a career. *The Australian*. Accessed at www .theaustralian.com.au/national-affairs/education/daggy -tag-turning-school-leavers-off-teaching-as-a-career/story -fn59nlz9-1227270128300 on April 6, 2015.

Busteed, B. (2013). *The school cliff: Student engagement drops with each school year*. Accessed at www.gallup.com/opinion/gallup/170525 /school-cliff-student-engagement-drops-school-year.aspx on April 6, 2015.

Carter, J. S. (2015, March 27). *Breaking the ruler: Melbourne school lets students choose when to learn, what to study*. Accessed at www .abc.net.au/radionational/programs/rnafternoons/victorian-high -school-teaching-a-new-way/6353574 on April 6, 2015.

Chao, R. O., & Lopez-Gottardi, C. (2015, March 19). How America's education model kills creativity and entrepreneurship. *Forbes*. Accessed at www.forbes.com/sites/darden/2015/03/19/how -americas-education-model-kills-creativity-and-entrepreneurship-2 on April 6, 2015.

Conklin, H. G. (2015, March 3). Playtime isn't just for preschoolers—Teenagers need it, too. *TIME*. Accessed at http://time.com/3726098/learning-through-play-teenagers-education on April 6, 2015.

Cormier, D. (2014, December 30). *There's something wrong in education: A response to Stephen Downes.* Accessed at http://davecormier.com/edblog/2014/12/30/theres-something-wrong-in-education-a-response-to-stephen-downes on April 6, 2015.

CV Mosaic Collective. (n.d.). *About.* Accessed at www.cvmosaic.org/about.html on April 7, 2015.

Dixon, B. (in press). *The end of school as we know it.* Bloomington, IN: Solution Tree Press.

Dixon, B., & Einhorn, S. (2011, June 15). *The right to learn: Identifying precedents for sustainable change.* Bellevue, WA: Anytime Anywhere Learning Foundation.

Elmore, R. F. (2015, January 5). The future is learning, but what about schooling? *Inside Higher Ed.* Accessed at www.insidehighered.com/blogs/higher-ed-beta/future-learning-what-about-schooling on April 6, 2015.

Engel, S. (2015). *The hungry mind: The origins of curiosity in childhood.* Cambridge, MA: Harvard University Press.

Garner, R. (2015, March 25). Finland schools: Subjects scrapped and replaced with 'topics' as country reforms its education system. *The Independent.* Accessed at www.redicecreations.com/article.php?id=32969 on April 6, 2015.

Government of Alberta. (2014). *Why Inspiring Education?* Accessed at http://inspiring.education.alberta.ca/what-is-inspiring-education/why-inspiring-education on April 10, 2015.

Grasgreen, A. (2014, February 26). Ready or not. *Inside Higher Ed.* Accessed at www.insidehighered.com/news/2014/02/26/provosts-business-leaders-disagree-graduates-career-readiness on April 6, 2015.

Gray, P. (2012, September 17). As children's freedom has declined, so has their creativity. *Psychology Today*. Accessed at www .psychologytoday.com/blog/freedom-learn/201209/children-s -freedom-has-declined-so-has-their-creativity on April 6, 2015.

Halpern, R., Heckman, P., & Larson, R. (2013). *Realizing the potential of learning in middle adolescence*. Accessed at www .howyouthlearn.org/pdf/Realizing%20the%20Poential%20 of%20Learning%20in%20Middle%20Adolescence.pdf on April 6, 2015.

Hardy, M. (2010). *Detox process: The what* [Video file]. Accessed at www.slideshare.net/monk51295/process-for-slideshare?ref =http://labconnections.blogspot.com/p/detox.html on April 5, 2015.

Hartkamp, C. (2014). Sudbury schools and democratic education in Knowmad Society. In J. W. Moravec (Ed.), *Knowmad Society* (pp. 129–162). Minneapolis, MN: Education Futures.

Holt, J. (1974). *Escape from childhood*. New York: Dutton.

Illich, I. (1971). *Deschooling society*. New York: Harper & Row.

Jenkins, L. (2012). Reversing the downside of student enthusiasm. *School Administrator, 5*(69), 16–17. Accessed at www.aasa.org /content.aspx?id=23242 on April 6, 2015.

Juliani, A. J. (2015). *Inquiry and innovation in the classroom: Using 20% time, genius hour, and PBL to drive student success*. New York: Routledge.

Kamenetz, A. (2010). *DIY U: Edupunks, edupreneurs, and the coming transformation of higher education*. White River Junction, VT: Chelsea Green.

Kamenetz, A. (2014). How engaged are students and teachers in American schools? *MindShift*. Accessed at ww2.kqed.org/mindshift /2014/04/15/how-engaged-are-students-and-teachers-in-american -schools on April 10, 2015.

Mandel, J. (2014). Welders make $150,000? Bring back shop class. *Wall Street Journal*. Accessed at www.wsj.com/articles/SB1000142 4052702303663604579501801872226532 on June 9, 2015.

McClintock, R. (2015, February 3). *Mosaic development, our working "bio."* Accessed at http://vivsoninteractive.com/?p=768 on April 6, 2015.

Moravec, J. W. (2014). *Knowmad Society*. Minneapolis, MN: Education Futures.

Nott, R. (2015). Brief tenure not unusual for superintendents. *Santa Fe New Mexican*. Accessed at www.santafenewmexican.com/news /education/brief-tenure-not-unusual-for-superintendents/article _48ad9ce3-1d55-52f1-aeed-14ffa30a0600.html on June 9, 2015.

Ombelets, J. (2014). Enhancing the talent pipeline. *Northeastern Magazine*. Accessed at www.northeastern.edu/magazine /enhancing-the-talent-pipeline on April 6, 2015.

Papert, S. (1993). *The children's machine: Rethinking school in the age of the computer*. New York: Basic Books.

Perkins, D. N. (2014). *Future wise: Educating our children for a changing world*. San Francisco: Jossey-Bass.

Postman, N. (1969). *The three I program: "Postman proposal," 1969*. Accessed at http://foody.org/3i/proposal1969.html on April 7, 2015.

Preiss, B. (2014, September 7). Templestowe school in a class of its own. *The Age*. Accessed at www.theage.com.au/victoria /templestowe-school-in-a-class-of-its-own-20140906-10c6tp .html on April 6, 2015.

Quinn, D. (2000). *Schooling: The hidden agenda*. Accessed at www .naturalchild.org/guest/daniel_quinn.html on April 7, 2015.

Richardson, W. (2015, March 18). *Still here . . . sort of.* Accessed at http://willrichardson.com/post/113964746960/still-here-sort-of on April 7, 2015.

Samuelson, K. (2012). Study puts average college debt at $40,000. *Chicago Tribune.* Accessed at http://articles.chicagotribune.com /2012-07-13/business/chi-study-puts-average-college-debt-at -40000-20120713_1_student-debt-student-loans-graduates on June 9, 2015.

Sappir, M. (2009). Sudbury Schools. *Did You Learn Anything?* Accessed at www.didyoulearnanything.net/about/sudbury on June 9, 2015.

Schank, R. C. (2011). *Teaching minds: How cognitive science can save our schools.* New York: Teachers College Press.

Schank, R. C. (in press). *Make school meaningful—and fun!* Bloomington, IN: Solution Tree Press.

Schneider, M. (2014). What is mosaic? *The Collaboraider.* Accessed at http://collaboraider.com/post/69395741424/what-is-mosaic on April 7, 2015.

Shaffer, K. (2015). *Academic freedom is for students, too.* Accessed at http://kris.shaffermusic.com/2015/04/academic-freedom-is-for -students on June 9, 2015.

Simon, S. (2015, February 10). No profit left behind. *POLITICO.* Accessed at www.politico.com/story/2015/02/pearson-education -115026.html on April 7, 2015.

Smith, F. (1998). *The book of learning and forgetting.* New York: Teachers College Press.

Socol, I. (2009, May 28). *Great schools: 1. Changing everything.* Accessed at http://speedchange.blogspot.com /2009/05/great-schools-1-changing-everything.html on April 7, 2015.

Stager, G. (n.d.). A good prompt is worth 1,000 words. *Creative Educator.* Accessed at http://creativeeducator.tech4learning.com /2012/articles/A_Good_Prompt_is_Worth_1000_Words on April 10, 2015.

Strauss, V. (2015, March 30). Report: Big education firms spend millions lobbying for pro-testing policies. *Washington Post.* Accessed at www.washingtonpost.com/blogs/answer-sheet/wp/2015/03/30/report-big-education-firms-spend-millions-lobbying-for-pro-testing-policies on April 10, 2015.

Tallgrass Sudbury School. (n.d.). *The philosophy.* Accessed at www.tallgrasssudbury.org/the-philosophy on April 10, 2015.

Tate, R. (2013). Google couldn't kill 20 percent time even if it wanted to. *Wired.* Accessed at www.wired.com/2013/08/20-percent-time-will-never-die on June 9, 2015.

Vangelova, L. (2014, October 10). How students lead the learning experience at Democratic schools. *MindShift.* Accessed at ww2.kqed.org/mindshift/2014/10/10/students-lead-the-learning-experience-at-democratic-schools on April 10, 2015.

Weigel, M., James, C., & Gardner, H. (2009). Learning: Peering backward and looking forward in the digital era. *International Journal of Learning and Media, 1*(1). Accessed at www.mitpressjournals.org/doi/pdf/10.1162/ijlm.2009.0005 on April 6, 2015.

Westervelt, E. (2015, March 3). *Where have all the teachers gone?* Accessed at www.npr.org/blogs/ed/2015/03/03/389282733/where-have-all-the-teachers-gone on April 10, 2015.

Solutions for Modern Learning

Solutions Series: Solutions for Modern Learning engages K–12 educators in a powerful conversation about learning and schooling in the connected world. In a short, reader-friendly format, these books challenge traditional thinking about education and help to develop the modern contexts teachers and leaders need to effectively support digital learners.

Claim Your Domain—And Own Your Online Presence
Audrey Watters
BKF687

The End of School as We Know It
Bruce Dixon
BKF692

Freedom to Learn
Will Richardson
BKF688

Gearing Up for Learning Beyond K–12
Bryan Alexander
BKF693

Make School Meaningful—And Fun!
Roger C. Schank
BKF686

The New Pillars of Modern Teaching
Gayle Allen
BKF685

Wait! Your professional development journey doesn't have to end with the last pages of this book.

We realize improving student learning doesn't happen overnight. And your school or district shouldn't be left to puzzle out all the details of this process alone.

No matter where you are on the journey, we're committed to helping you get to the next stage.

Take advantage of everything from **custom workshops** to **keynote presentations** and **interactive web and video conferencing**. We can even help you develop an action plan tailored to fit your specific needs.

Let's get the conversation started.

Call 888.763.9045 today.

solution-tree.com